Educating girl child: Importance of educating the girl child and adding value to life

(Elizabeth B. Caron)

Caron),
(2022).

Table of contents

Chapter 1

Girls' Education

Every day, girls encounter challenges to attending school due to poverty, cultural norms and practices, insufficient infrastructure, violence and fragility. Girls' education is a strategic development objective for the World Bank.

Ensuring that all girls and young women obtain a decent education is their human right, a global development objective, and a strategic focus for the World Bank.

Achieving gender equality is key to the World Bank Group's core aims of eradicating extreme poverty and building shared prosperity. As the biggest financial development partner in education worldwide, the World Bank guarantees that all of its education initiatives are gender-sensitive and helps to address obstacles that are preventing girls and boys from equitably benefiting from countries' investments in education.

Females' education

extends beyond getting girls into school. It is also about ensuring that girls learn and feel safe while in school; have the opportunity to complete all levels of education, acquiring the knowledge and skills to compete in the labor market; gain socio-emotional and life skills necessary to navigate and adapt to a changing world; make decisions about their own lives; and contribute to their communities and the world.

Both people and nations gain from

girls' education. Better educated women tend to be better informed about diet and healthcare, have fewer children, marry at a later age, and their children are typically healthier, should they choose to become moms. They are more likely to join the formal job market and earn greater salaries.

A recent World Bank analysis predicts that the "limited educational options for females, and hurdles to completing 12 years of school, cost nations between US

$15 trillion and $30 trillion in lost lifetime output and earnings." All these elements together may help pull homes, communities, and nations out of poverty.

The Challenge According to UNESCO estimates,

throughout the globe, 129 million females are out of school, including 32 million of primary school age and 97 million of secondary school age.

Globally, primary and secondary school enrolment rates are growing closer to equal for girls and boys (90 percent male, 89 percent female) (90 percent male, 89 percent female).

But while enrollment rates are similar—in fact, two-thirds of all countries have reached gender parity in primary school enrollment—completion rates for girls are lower in low-income countries, where 63 percent of female primary school students complete primary school, compared to 67 percent of male primary school students.

In low-income nations, secondary school completion rates for females also continue to lag, with just 36 percent of girls finishing lower secondary school compared to 44 percent of boys. Upper secondary completion rates exhibit comparable inequalities in lower income nations. The figure is 26 percent for young males and 21 percent for young women.

The inequalities are starker in nations afflicted by fragility, conflict, and violence

(FCV) (FCV). Females are 2.5 times more likely than boys to be absent from school in FCV countries, and at the secondary level, they are 90 percent more likely to be absent than those in non-FCV situations.

Both girls and boys are

confronting a learning crisis. Learning Poverty (LP) estimates the fraction of children who are not able to read fluently at age 10. While females are 4 percentage points less learning-poor than boys, the percentages for both groups remain relatively high. In low- and middle-income countries, the average rate of learning is 55% for girls and 59% for men.

The disparity is smaller in low-income countries, where learning, poverty affects both boys and girls at roughly the same rate. In many nations, participation in postsecondary education somewhat benefits young women, but greater learning achievements do not translate into better career and life outcomes for women.

There is a huge gender discrepancy in labor force participation rates internationally.

It is especially noticeable in countries such as South Asia and the Middle East and North Africa, where female labor force participation rates are among the lowest, at 24 percent and 20 percent, respectively.

These are shockingly low rates when compared to Latin America (53 percent) and East Asia (59 percent), which are still lower than male rates.

Gender bias inside schools and classrooms may also reinforce messages that impact girls' objectives, their own views of their responsibilities in society, and cause labor market involvement gaps and occupational segregation.

When gender stereotypes are communicated through the design of school and classroom learning environments or through the behavior of faculty, staff, and peers in a child's school, it goes on to have a sustained impact on academic

performance
and choice of
field of study,
especially
negatively
affecting
young women
pursuing
science,
technology,
engineering,
and
mathematics
disciplines.

Poverty is one
of the most
crucial
variables in
deciding
whether a girl

can access and finish her education. Studies regularly suggest that girls who suffer from various obstacles — such as poor family income, living in distant or underserved places, or who have a handicap or belong to a minority ethno-linguist

ic group —
are far behind
in terms of
access to and
completion of
school.

Abuse also
prohibits girls
from
accessing and
finishing
education—so
metimes girls
are forced to
travel great
distances to
school,
putting them
at a higher
risk of

violence, and many suffer violence while at school. Most current research shows that over 60 million girls are sexually abused on their way to or at school every year.

This typically has major effects on their mental and physical health and general well-being, while also leading to reduced attendance and greater dropout rates. An estimated 246 million children face abuse in and around school every year. Eradicating school-related gender-based violence is crucial.

Adolescent pregnancies may be a consequence of sexual assault or sexual exploitation.

Girls who get pregnant frequently endure tremendous shame, and even prejudice, from their communities. The weight of shame,

exacerbated
by skewed
gender
standards,
may force
girls to drop
out of school
early and not
return.

Child
marriage is
also a serious
concern. Girls
who marry
early are far
more likely to
drop out of
school and
finish fewer
years of

schooling than their counterparts who marry later. They are also more likely to have children at a young age and are subjected to greater levels of violence committed by their spouse.

In turn, this impacts the education and health of their

children, as
well as their
capacity to
make a
livelihood.
Females with
a secondary
education are
up to six
times more
likely to
marry than
children with
little or no
education.Acc
ording to a
recent survey,
more than
41,000
females
under the age

of 18 get married every day. Putting a halt to this practice would enhance women's predicted educational achievement and, with it, their prospective incomes. According to the report's estimations, stopping child marriage may yield more than US $500 billion in benefits yearly.

COVID-19 is having a detrimental effect on girls' health and well-being, and many are at danger of not returning to school once they reopen. Available evidence demonstrates that the incidence of violence against girls and women has grown throughout the epidemic, compromising their health, safety and general well-being. As school closures and quarantines were imposed during the 2014–2016 Ebola epidemic in West Africa, women and girls endured increasing sexual abuse, coercion, and exploitation.

School closures during the Ebola epidemic were connected with an increase in adolescent pregnancies.

Once schools reopened, several "visibly pregnant girls" were prevented from coming back to school.

With schools closing throughout the developing world, where stigma around teenage pregnancies prevails, we will probably see an increase in drop-out rates as teenage girls become pregnant or married. As girls stay at home because of school closures, their household work burdens might increase, resulting in girls spending more time helping out at home instead of studying.

This might encourage parents, particularly those putting a lower value on girls' education, to keep their daughters at home even after schools reopen. Moreover, research shows that girls risk dropping out of school when caregivers are missing from the household because they typically have to (partly) replace the work done by the missing caregiver, who might be away due to COVID-19-related work, illness, or death.

Therefore, with the present COVID-19 epidemic, we could see more girls than boys assisting at home, trailing behind with studying, and dropping out of school.

Count me in! Improving Education Outcomes for Girls and

Young Women,
World Bank
Education
Ensuring that
all girls and
young women
receive a
quality
education is
their human
right, a global
development
priority, and
a strategic
priority for
the World
Bank.

Chapter 2

Importance of girl child education:

Biological female offspring from birth to 18 years of age. This is the age before one becomes a young adult.

This era encompasses the creche, nursery or early childhood (0–5 years), primary (6–12 years) and secondary (12–18 years) (12–18 years). During this stage, the small kid is fully in the care of the adult, who may be their parents or guardian.

Which suggests she is reliant on the importance of others. Education is the process of delivering knowledge to an inexperienced individual to help him or her improve physically,

cognitively,
socially,
emotionally,
spiritually,
politically,
and
economically.
Education is
the process
by which
people
become
effective
members of
their
community
(Ocho 2005).
(Ocho 2005).

It is a process
by which a

person gets information and discovers his or her potentialities and utilizes them for self-actualizat ion and to be beneficial to others. It is a way of conserving, disseminating , and enhancing the culture of a civilization.

To educate a female kid is

to cultivate her brains, character, and talents. Education is a crucial human right that should be given to every kid irrespective of age and nationality. The importance of education in the lives of girls cannot be overstated.Education is essential in both the spiritual and temporal aspects of our lives.light that illuminates the path by dispelling the darkness of ignorance; salt that offers the flavor of life; the medication that heals; and the key that unlocks doors. The greatest gift a girl child can receive is education and the ability to educate others.

According to a Chinese saying, education is the best legacy to offer a kid since providing your child a skill is better than giving him or her a thousand pieces of cash.

Many females nowadays do not have appropriate schooling above a particular age. The local traditional view is that a woman's place is in her husband's kitchen and her principal function is in her house.

This notion
has kept
many girls
away from
school.

When a girl is
given out in
marriage at a
very delicate
age, her right
as a human
has been
violated. She
has also been
denied her
right to
education
and will be
destined to
remain

illiterate forever if her husband does not offer her access to school.

It has been proved by academics that supporting female education is vital for national development, and the contribution of women cannot be overlooked. The usual notion is that when you educate a man, you educate one, but when you teach a woman, you educate a country.

This is so because the education of every kid begins at home, and the mother is the first teacher.

Educating the female child generates women who are educated and will, in turn, educate their children, care for their family, and provide for their children.

Therefore, educating the female child leads to improved health for future generations, a decrease in child mobility and mortality, thereby sparking a snowball effect of attaining all other sustainable development objectives in a practical way. The female child's education also prepares her to confront realities in society and trains her to be a decent wife and mother.

When she gets educated, she understands the entire potential implanted in her; she discovers that she can be whatever and whatever she wants to be.

With education, she would crack the shell of ignorance and uncover the treasure of self-discovery.

The children's right act should be reinforced and implemented in all states. This will go a long way towards checking indiscriminate child maltreatment.

Policymakers must also provide an enabling climate for boosting gender engagement in creating a vital conduit for the educated girl child to be turned into a woman who will be agents of national development.

The Importance of Girl Child Education in Our Societyby Ajay Singh | April 3, 2021 Educating the female child leads to every aspect of education that works to enhance the ability and experience of girls.

This encompasses general education at schools and colleges; professional education; vocational education; technical education; etc. I know the significance of female child education in our culture. Education is a fundamental aspect of a living human, whether it is a boy or a girl. Education enables a person to be wiser, to discover new things, and to know about the facts around the world.

Education is recognized to be the cornerstone of our society since it is one of the fastest and most effective ways of stimulating economic progress in any country. It is believed to be the primary key to ending poverty and crime against girls.

Educating the girls of a country from the top schools in

India also boosts children's and women's endurance rates and health difficulties, prevents child marriage, empowers women both in their career and also at home, and aids in coping with climate change. An educated woman may educate her whole family.

For the advancement of Indian society or the whole planet, women should be properly educated. On some days, for the growth of India and Indian society, women are working better. In every zone of development, education is extremely crucial. Understanding the relevance of women's education, the government and numerous non-government groups took on many programs to improve women's education. So now we will know the value of female education.

Let Us Examine the Importance of Girl Children Education in Our Society:
1. Aid in the Development of More Stable Communities To Assist In Building

More Stable Communities Education brings strength and adaptability, which helps the country grow at a faster pace from any disagreement. The overall quality of education may even aid in avoiding arguments in the first place by imparting information on social skills, problem-solving, and critical thinking at schools. And, while primary education is critical for females, secondary education may be a game changer in their lives.

2.Promote Gender Equality

In today's culture, gender equality continues to be a widespread concern because of the ongoing imbalance in terms of access to opportunities for women and men. Gender equality is a core human right that every human being is entitled to regardless of color, sexuality, nationality, or religion. As a consequence, the role men and women play in society is entirely established, and as a consequence, there is a gender disparity. When women in our society are better educated, greater influence is exerted on gender equality.

Since women attained equality, human rights have become a strong value in society, as women in government prefer to advocate for impoverished groups.

Women's leadership in government is also becoming more common, and when women lead, they advocate for more unbiased principles of governance.

3. Allow Girls to Make Their Own Choices. Females who are educated have more

courage and freedom to make decisions that affect their lives.They are better encouraged to analyze the societal need for women to live in the home, developing children and undertaking the ordinary chores. Education from the greatest institutions in India encourages young women to look beyond cultural boundaries and continue their ambitions for a better life.

4. Stimulates economies and advances the fight to eradicate poverty
One of the clearest and

most evident advantages of teaching female students from the top schools in India is the promise of the economic growth of a nation.

The comparable occurrence influences the country's Gross Domestic Product

(GDP) rate with a rise in women's education involvement. When the women of a nation are taught and educated, the entire economy thrives and flourishes.

5. Positive Change for Future Generations Positive Change for

Future
Generations
The educated
girl becomes
an educated
lady.

Offering girls
an education
is a vital step
in producing
future
generations
of healthy,
educated, and
powerful
females.
Educated
women in the
community
may become

future leaders, steer towards change, and construct more strong and important societies. And consequently, a country is seen only as prosperous because of its population.

6. Option to Pursue a Career of Her Choice

It is one of the most important aspects of female child education.The educated women may be shown to be powerful in their various occupations. When a female child has the opportunity to be educated, she has a better chance of becoming a successful engineer, doctor, or whatever job she desires.

7. Better Life And Health

Chapter 3

Improved Life And Health

Educating female children contributes to the development of a decent life. The girl can read and learn about her rights. They won't be stomped down over her rights.

There will be an overall improvement in their lives. Educated females provide knowledge of the significance of health and cleanliness. Through teaching, they may lead a healthy lifestyle.

Child education is one of the most significant topics. Every girl in our society must have the right to be educated since education is the most important and crucial weapon that can be utilized to overcome the issues of human life.

When teaching a female child: Even though in 2014, approximatel y 15% of women worldwide are unable to read or write.That's approximately 500 million women. But this is not simply an issue for them. It's a dilemma for all of us. Because whether a girl, boy, man, or woman, we all live in the

same world,
and that
world needs
all the brain
capacity,
creativity,
and
productivity
it can get. It
requires
today's
females to
rise to their
potential.

Over the last
several
weeks, my
colleagues at
Brookings
have

published a
series of blog
entries on
girls'
education
and the issues
facing it
throughout
the globe.

Authors
included
Judith-Ann
Walker of
Nigeria,
Urvashi Sahni
of India and
Khadim
Hussein of
Pakistan, all
of whom

shared
compelling,
moving
experiences
of their work
with girls in
their own
countries and
the
troublesome
challenges
and amazing
benefits that
have come
with it. We're
also having
an event here
at Brookings
on June 17,
which will
feature a talk

by U.SGlobal Ambassador for Women and Girls Catherine Russell and a panel on emerging methods within the sector.

 I will conduct the second and final panel, which will discuss how individuals can and do give leadership in this area to those who most need it. But for now, I want to just address the question: why is this topic so crucial for everyone?

Three reasons:

Educating women boosts the economy. Additional education increases career opportunities for women but also helps generate jobs for everyone and promotes the economy. Any economist will tell you that people are resources—or human capital—and if we don't educate the full half of them who are women, we are losing out on a great chance for a richer and more productive society.

For example, in sub-Saharan Africa, investing in girls' education might raise agricultural productivity by 25 percent, creating economic development and providing more food for the entire continent.

Educating women promotes health—for everyone. Better educated moms are more likely to seek care when their children are unwell. In underdeveloped nations,

people are
more likely to
cleanse their
water.
Education
helps moms
know how to
nourish their
children with
healthy
nutrition, and
it decreases
child
mortality
rates.

But the
advantages of
educated
women do
not end with

their offspring. One estimate says that if all women had a secondary education, vaccines in poor and lower-middle income countries would rise by 43 percent. This enhances the health and safety of large communities, indeed our whole globe, since it implies that fewer individuals will carry and transmit illness.

Educating women is beneficial for our environment. In the same way that education can increase the economy by improving agricultural yields, it can

conserve
water by
permitting
smart,
effective
irrigation.
Indeed,
education
may lead to a
more efficient
use of all
resources.

A study of 29
nations
indicated that
although only
25 percent of
people with
just a basic
education

express concern for the environment, 46 percent of those with more than a high school degree do. And, while this data shows that education is important for both girls and boys, the return on investment may be more obvious for females, who are currently underserved. When an educated girl grows up to be an educated woman, the benefits are felt by their colleagues, partners, children, and friends, often leading to better environmental consciousness among a large array of people.

These facts are powerful. They illustrate that girls' education is not merely a problem for girls themselves or even their enthusiastic supporters. When Judith-Ann Walker talks about educating females in northeast Nigeria, she is also talking about Nigeria's economy. When Urvashi Sahni speaks about the schooling issues confronting Indian females, she is also talking about the health of the whole nation. And when Khadim

Hussein talks about the potential to promote girls' education in Pakistan, he is talking about the country's environment too.

Girls' education is a concern for everyone. Improving it should be—and is—important for all of us.

Educating girls means investing in a critical, overlooked, and underused element of our society, and that investment will lead to a healthier and richer world. girl-child education